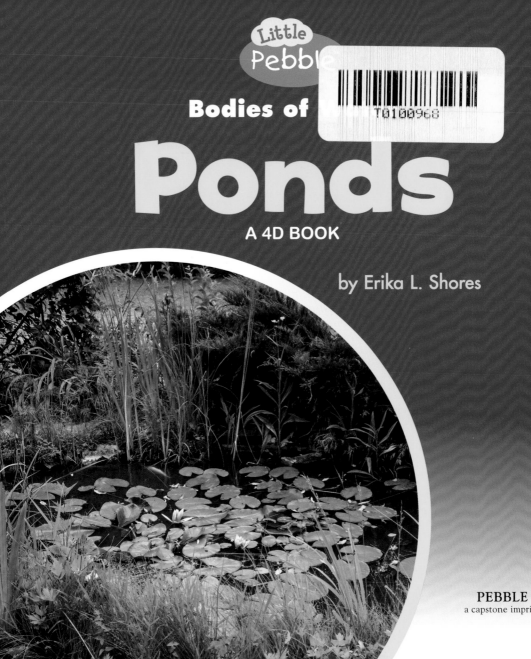

Little
Pebble

Bodies of Water

T0100968

Ponds

A 4D BOOK

by Erika L. Shores

PEBBLE
a capstone imprint

Download the Capstone 4D™ app!

- Ask an adult to download the Capstone 4D app.
- Scan the cover and stars inside the book for additional content.

When you scan a spread, you'll find fun extra stuff to go with this book! You can also find these things on the web at www.capstone4D.com using the password: ponds.14667

Little Pebble is published by Pebble
1710 Roe Crest Drive, North Mankato,
Minnesota 56003
www.mycapstone.com

Library of Congress Cataloging-in-Publication Data
Library of Congress Cataloging-in-Publication Data is available on the Library of Congress website.
ISBN: 978-1-5435-1466-7 (library binding)—
978-1-5435-1470-4 (paperback)—
978-1-5435-1474-2 (ebook PDF)

Editorial Credits
Bobbie Nuytten, designer; Morgan Walters, media researcher; Tori Abraham, production specialist

Photo Credits
Alamy: Design Pics Inc, 21, F1online digitale Bildagentur GmbH, 19; Shutterstock: BBA Photography, 9, Elena Elisseeva, Cover, 1, Ethan Daniels, 14, Iness Arna, 5, 15, Ivanita2017, 13, kavram, 7, Proskurina Yuliya, (wave) design element, S.Z., 11, silvergull, 17

Printed and bound in China.
000309

Table of Contents

What Is a Pond?

A pond is a small body
of water. It has land
on all its sides.

Ponds are 12 to 15 feet (4 to 5 meters) deep. Lakes are much deeper.

Freshwater fills ponds.

The water is still.

What Is in a Pond?

Algae grow in ponds. These tiny plants do not have roots.

Say algae (al-GEE)

algae

Look!

Snails eat

the tiny plants.

The sun shines.

Its rays reach the bottom.

This helps plants

with roots grow.

Frogs lay eggs
on plants.

eggs

Flies buzz.

Snap!

Frogs eat pond insects.

People and Ponds

It's winter.

Pond water freezes.

People skate on the ice.

Glossary

algae—small plants without roots or stems that grow in water

freshwater—water that is found in ponds, lakes, and rivers

insect—a small animal with a hard outer shell, six legs, three body sections, and two antennae; most insects have wings.

root—the part of the plant that is underground

snail—a small animal with no legs, a soft, slimy body, and a shell on its back

still—quiet, calm, or without motion

Read More

Benjamin, Tina. *Let's Go to a Pond*. Let's Go Outdoors. New York: Gareth Stevens Publishing, 2016.

Kopp, Megan. *What Do You Find in a Pond?* Ecosystems Close-Up. New York: Crabtree Publishing Company, 2016.

Rustad, Martha E. H. *What's in a Pond?* What's in There? North Mankato, Minn.: Capstone Press, 2016.

Internet Sites

Use FactHound to find Internet sites related to this book.

Visit www.facthound.com

Just type in 9781543514667 and go.

Super-cool stuff!

Check out projects, games and lots more at
www.capstonekids.com

Critical Thinking Questions

1. What is the difference between a pond and a lake?

2. What do snails eat in a pond?

3. What happens to pond water in winter when it is very cold outside?

Index